A Mother's
PRAYERS

Rita Kitchen

WESTBOW
PRESS®
A DIVISION OF THOMAS NELSON
& ZONDERVAN

WestBow Press books may be ordered through booksellers or by contacting:

WestBow Press
A Division of Thomas Nelson & Zondervan
1663 Liberty Drive
Bloomington, IN 47403
www.westbowpress.com
1 (866) 928-1240

ISBN: 978-1-5127-5720-0 (sc)
ISBN: 978-1-5127-5721-7 (e)

Print information available on the last page.

WestBow Press rev. date: 9/28/2016

This book is dedicated to three extraordinary women that I have been honored to have in my life.

My mother, Juanita, is a strong Christian woman that has given me love and guidance always.

My maternal grandmother, Bonnie.
My paternal grandmother, Bivian.

Both of my grandmothers were very different but the same because they both were Christian women. I continue to think of them often and how much they loved their families and God.

My love to you always,
Rita Kay

Contents

Prayer

*Pray without ceasing – (*First Thessalonians 5:17) (King James Version)

Prayer is an essential part of our daily lives. Praying nourishes our soul and gives us peace and comfort. I have often thought about how do I pray? I am sure that you have wondered about it also.

But when ye pray, use not vain repetitions, as the heathen do; for they think that they shall be heard for their much speaking. (Matthew 6:7)

You do not want to use flowery words just because it sounds pretty and makes a person sound intelligent. God wants us to come to Him with our praises, thanksgiving, concerns and problems with a sincere heart.

*Be careful for nothing; but in every thing by prayer and supplication with thanksgiving let your request be made known unto God. (*Philippians 4:6)

In this book I have included different subjects that we as mothers might encounter. There is no way to cover every subject, thought or idea. The prayers listed in this book are situations from my own personal experiences, from my observations of family and friends and some of the subjects are not about either but from things I have learned regarding what to pray for. Sometimes we do not think about all the different things we should pray about because we find ourselves so busy that we only pray when we have a problem or in praise when we get something wonderful.

Children learn not only by our words but also our actions. Our lives as mothers encompass many areas. We have our relationship with our parents, our husband, our extended family and our children. We also encounter other people in our lives such as friends, co-workers, church and even the people we meet in the grocery store. Our children are watching how we interact with each person. Then there are social issues and general things such as how we think about a variety of subjects that our children are watching us and learning from our actions and how we react. Do we make mistakes? Yes, and lots of them. We may not respond in the right way to every situation. The important thing is to learn from our mistakes and moving forward that we do not repeat those mistakes. We can also learn from others mistakes. If I see things that others say and do and I think about how that mistake looks and how it makes that other person look. Then I have learned something.

I am not saying that I have all the answers because I don't. None of us are perfect. The sections in this book are things that we all encounter not only as mothers but just because we are people. I am not saying that I know everything about each subject and I don't claim to be an expert in any of the subject matters listed. I am saying I have learned some things and still have a lot to learn. You may wonder about my credentials for writing this book. The answer is none. I do not have a degree in Theology. I have not attended Seminary. I have a degree in Business. The only thing I have to offer is that I feel led by God to write this book. I continue to pray that God will give me the words that He would have me to say. I hope this book will help someone and that they may receive comfort and strength in their daily walk with God. I pray that this book will give God all the glory and praise.

I ask that you use these prayers as a guideline during your prayer time. This book is meant to make each reader reflect on their prayer life.

Come with me on this journey of motherhood and prayer. May we grow together!

The Mother's Prayer

Lo, children are an heritage of the Lord: and the fruit of the womb is his reward. (Psalm 127:3)

Becoming a mother was the most thrilling and scariest time of my life. I was over joyed when I became a mother. I was terrified. I wanted to do everything right but constantly falling short. No matter how hard you try to do everything right we just cannot do it. It is not realistic. However, we must always try very hard every day to be the best mother we can possibly be.

Changing a diaper, preparing a bottle, getting them to school, taking them to sports practice and games is the easiest part. The challenge is to learn each child's personality. By that statement I mean, each child likes different foods, different colors, and different toys and has different needs. Some children like to play outside while some prefer to stay inside to read and watch television. Some children love going to school while another hates it. One child may be a social butterfly and another may be a loner. Some children are stubborn while others are happy go lucky. Some children have a pleasant personality while another is difficult to get along with them. One child may obey easily while the other challenges your every statement. Learning all these things about our children improves our ability to communicate with them. Once we understand each child's personality, we can relate to them on an astounding level. You will be beyond delighted with your communication. Each day will be promising and you will have a new perspective on your child.

At each stage in our children's lives we change gears so to speak. Our prayers are adjusted as well. The early years of formula, diapers and playing we pray that we survive and our sweet bundle of joy too because we don't know what we are doing, especially if it is the first child. We pray that we don't drop them. We are constantly concerned about every little sniffle. Then there is the twelve years of school and that requires our patience to be kicked up several notches. The homework, their friends, school activities, sports and everything else that comes along. It keeps us busy but it is also a wonderful time. Our children's lives are being molded in what we hope will become a well- rounded individual. We pray that we get them through the school years. Now they are adults but they are still our babies. They need guidance in college, jobs and relationships. Our prayer changes again for the grown up child. Young adults experience life completely different than when I was in my late teens and early twenty's. The world today is super competitive and nothing seems simple. We pray that we know how to guide.

I have heard about two similar situations regarding a mother daughter relationship that I want to share. Now I do not know either of these families but have friends and family that know them. The mother in both situations has done everything for their daughters. They did not teach their daughters how to take care of themselves.

One daughter headed off to college and went into a gigantic panic attack. She went into a panic about driving around town because her mother never encouraged her to drive on her own. The girl did not know how to pick out her clothes because her mother always helped her decide what she would wear. The girl did not know how to do anything. I assume the mother thought she was showing her daughter how much she loved her by doing everything for her but she actually has done her daughter a huge disservice. Proof of that is that the girl went into a panic when she was on her own at college. She did not know how to make a decision without her mother.

The other mother was a stay at home mother and she never taught her daughter how to wash dishes, do laundry or any household chores. The daughter does not know how to do anything. The person that told me this story said the girl has no motivation to start anything to improve her life. She seemed to not know how to take care of basic needs in her life and did not understand how to apply to college nor how to go about applying for a job. The girl had not been taught anything to help her get started at being an adult. In both situation the mothers did not teach their daughters how to take care of themselves.

Regardless of the stage in our child's life, it is very important that we continue to seek God's guidance through prayer.

The Mother's Prayer

Dear God,

I give you all the praise and glory for entrusting me with the care and love of my children.

As a mother providing shelter, food and clothing is usually the easiest part of being a mother.

Caring for the mind and heart is the challenge.

Help me to not get so busy with daily chores that I forget to give hugs and kisses.

Help me to show unconditional love so they will learn to give and receive love.

Teach me to nurture them when they are sick so they will learn compassion.

Teach me to be kind to family and friends so they will learn kindness and to give with an open heart and to help those in need.

Give me the words to teach them about your Son, Jesus Christ so they may be saved.

Let my child learn to pray by my example

Teach me patience so they will learn tolerance

Teach me to be honest in all that I say and do so they will learn to trust.

Help me to remember to see the joy in all things so they will see beauty.

Humble my heart when someone has done me wrong so that I can forgive so they will learn forgiveness and have peace in their heart.

Teach me to be content with my blessings so they will learn joy

Teach me to smile and laugh everyday so they will learn to have laughter in their heart.

Teach me to give guidance so they will learn to make good solid decisions.

Teach me to listen to my children so they will feel valued and loved.

I ask these things in Jesus name.

Amen

A Prayer for our Children

Children, obey your parents in all things: for this is well pleasing unto the Lord. (Colossians 3:20)

When I brought my daughter home from the hospital, I looked at her and thought what do I do now? You think you are prepared but when you bring the baby home you feel that you are not ready for even the simplest things. About four years earlier, I had three surgeries on my wrists. My wrist were still weak when I had her and I was afraid that I would drop her. Thankfully I did not. There are fears that envelop your every waking moment. We make it through the infant and toddler stage. Yea, school time! There are new fears that wash over us. Can't we just keep them home where they are safe?

From the day we put them in kindergarten and until they graduate from high school, we are constantly concerned about their days in school. We are concerned about their learning. I would guess the things I learned in middle school, kids today learn those things in elementary school. The pressure to learn more and to learn it faster is put on our kids from day one. We are afraid that our child will not be able to keep up. Not every child will make straight A's. It is not realistic. Have you ever noticed that when you speak with someone that you have not seen in a while their child is the smartest in their class? Their child excels at everything. Every one brags about how smart their child is. Truth is not every child is smart. Your child will not shine at everything. Find what your child is good at and encourage them in that subject. If your child thrives in math and science, talk to them about those subjects and find out what inspires them. Discover what motivates them. It will direct them to a career that will be fulfilling.

Peer pressure can be beneficial to your child or it could lead them down a path of destruction. If your child has a friend that is great at science, then through peer pressure it makes your child want to participate perhaps in a science fair. That would be a good thing. On the other side of the coin peer pressure that your child's classmates might suggest he participate in could get him in trouble. The cool kids could pressure your child into doing drugs and because your child thinks they are popular and cool could make him fall victim to drug use.

It is our job as a mother to teach our children. We teach our children when we do not even realize we are teaching them. They see us prepare meals and it is teaching them that we care about their nourishment. We help them with their homework and we teach them that we care about their education. We may show them little tricks on how to memorize information for a test, how to spell words, how to research information or how to write a paper. Teach them the basics of life. Young children can pick up toys, put dirty laundry in the hamper or help feed and water the dog or cat. Older children can learn to do laundry, dishes or clean floors. As much as we love our babies we cannot do everything for them. We must teach them.

Then there are the hard life lessons that we need to teach. They may involve some tough love or something very simple. We discipline our children because we love them. We want them to be loving, kind, productive and well-rounded individuals. The question is when it comes to teaching our children life lessons, where do we draw the line between letting a child learn something the hard way or doing it for them?

Most people at some point in their life encounter bullies. For a child it can be traumatizing to be bullied at school or through social media. How should you as a mother handle the situation?

Do you let them figure it out or do you contact the school and intervene on their behalf. If you contact the school and solve their problem for them, the child can see it as either my mother does not think I am smart enough to handle this on my own or the child may love you all the more for helping them out. If you let them figure it out on their own the child could wonder why my mother doesn't help me out. It may make your child question your love for them. There is no correct answer. The best advice I can give on bullies is to know your child. Ask your child what he / she would like for you to do. If you happen to be the mother of a bully, I pray that you will consider counselling to help your child. We must pray that God will give us guidance on how to handle each situation.

Train up a child in the way he should go: and when he is old, he will not depart from it. (Proverbs 22:6)

There is pressure on kids to wear the latest and most fashionable clothes. Kids today have iPhones, iPads, and every year there is some new cool electronic gadget to capture our child's attention.

Children need to go outside and play. They need to ride their bike, climb a tree and play hide & go seek. They need to use their imagination.

Sports, dance, karate, music lessons, cheerleading are all fun activities. Children want to be a part of these activities because their friends are doing them. These should be fun but competitive. Children need the competition. It teaches them team work and boost their confidence.

A certain amount of stress for children is good because it motivates them. The problem comes in when it causes too much stress on a child. There is stress to be the brightest and best. What have we done as a society that has created such stress on our children?

We as mothers may feel overwhelmed by it all. We can be consumed with helping our child with homework, extra-curricular activities and spending quality time together that we may become stressed. We are adults and we feel stressed so as a child how can we expect them to handle it any better?

We are concerned with their self-esteem, confidence and their ability to cope day to day with life. A child may grow up with both sets of parents in the home, have good grades, involved in church, and have great friends and still struggle with self-esteem. They may believe that they are too tall or too short. They may feel they are fat. Kids may make fun of them for things that to us as an adult may seem silly but to a child it is serious. How are we to help our child?

If you are concerned about school, grades, stress, self-esteem and extracurricular activities for your child, I encourage you to take these concerns to God in prayer.

A Prayer for our Children

Dear God,

Thank you placing this bundle of joy in my life.

As my child heads for school I ask that you watch over and protect them.

I pray that they are not bullied nor will they become the bully.

I ask that my child has the ability to concentrate on the lesson that the teacher has planned.

I pray that the teacher comes to work today with a light heart and the desire to teach. I pray that the teacher teaches in a way that is good and right.

I pray that the teachers, administrators and staff are prepared to have my child in an environment that is safe.

I pray that each student be allowed to say the Pledge of Allegiance and congregate to have a time of prayer.

I ask that my child be respectful of all teachers.

I pray that my child be nice and kind to other students.

I pray that my child is happy and healthy.

I ask that my child be motivated and have self-esteem.

Each child is different, I pray that You will show me how to relate to my child so that I can help them grow and develop into the person that you would have them to be.

I ask these things in Jesus name.

Amen.

A Prayer for Listening

So that thou incline thine ear unto wisdom, and apply thine heart to understanding; (Proverbs 2:2)

How many times have we as parents said or thought oh she / he is just a child they don't know what they are talking about. I think all of us at one point have been guilty of doing this. Children want to be valued and heard. Otherwise they grow up believing that they are worthless and that their opinions do not matter.

The key to listening to your child is to know your child. That statement seems obvious but at times we need a gentle reminder of things we already know. When your baby cried you learned to distinguish between the cries. You knew a particular cry meant hunger another was my diaper needs changing and another was just please hold me. Well, when they get older and can talk to us we need to listen. I made a lot of mistakes in this area with my daughter. When she was a little girl she was afraid there was a monster under her bed. I did not listen. I thought she should know there are no such things as a monster under her bed. She was a little girl. I should have understood that she did not think like an adult. She thought like a child. I brushed it off. I was wrong because I did not listen to her.

Now as teenagers they may not want to talk to you but eventually they will and when they do we must listen. When your daughter is distraught because her boyfriend broke up with her, listen to her heartache. You may think she is only 16 and does not know what true love is because she is a child. For that 16 year old teenager, her heartache is very real. That is her realty. Listen to her anguish.

A Prayer for Listening

Dear God,

Thank you for your love. I ask that you teach me to listen to my children. Help me to respect their thoughts and opinions.

Help me to acknowledge their fears and heartaches. Help me to value the words that they say.

When my child comes to me with a problem show and teach me to listen to all that they say.

Help me to know when listening and a hug is enough and when I need to give guidance.

In Jesus name I pray.

Amen

A Prayer for Witnessing

Let your speech be alway with grace, seasoned with salt, that ye may know how ye ought to answer every man. (Colossians 4:6)

When we think about witnessing we usually think about talking to one or more people about the plan of salvation. We may talk to family, friends, coworkers or a stranger on the street. We may speak to them about Jesus dying on the cross for our sins but it is when we walk away from the conversation that shows our true witness. For example, if we are in a restaurant with someone and telling them about Jesus and how wonderful it is to have Him in our heart then the very next breath we speak to the waiter with a rude tone. We may have undone all that we have just said.

Does our actions match the words we speak? Everyone watches what we do and no one more than our children. What message does it send if you tell your daughter to be kind to her friends even though they are rude to her then she hears you be rude to your friends?

We all have bad days when we do not necessarily feel like being chipper and happy. However, it does not give us the right to be mean. Sometimes we are frustrated with a situation and we speak sharply before we even realize the words are out of our mouths. I have done this more times than I care to admit. We need to be mindful of how we speak to everyone. You never know when someone will hear you say something that you should not have said. They may comment,

"Did you hear her? I cannot believe she said that. Wow, I thought she was a Christian."

You want people to say, "Did you hear how nice she spoke to that person that was mean to her. Wow, she said she was a Christian. I guess she really is a true Christian. I want to be like her."

So many times we all fall short, I do so many times, but we should try to think about what we say and do because you never know when your actions will be the only witness someone may see.

But sanctify the Lord God in your hearts: and be ready always to give an answer to every man that asketh you a reason of the hope that is in you with meekness and fear: (1 Peter 3:15)

A Prayer for Witnessing

Dear God,

I ask that I be a witness for You.

Give me the right words so that someone will come to know Jesus as their Lord and Savior

Give me kind words to say so that family, friends and strangers will see You in all that I do. It is never my intention to hurt anyone. I never want to be mean.

I pray that my words and actions reflect a positive message to everyone that I come in contact with.

I pray that my children will be a witness for You in their actions and words.

In Jesus name I pray.

Amen.

The Friendship Prayer

A man that hath friends must shew himself friendly: and there is a friend that sticketh closer than a brother. (Proverbs 18:24)

The friends we choose can mean the difference between having a happy life or a life that is exhausting. Not many people have the same friends from grade school through their entire life. Most of us have had friends in high school then in college we make new friends. As our jobs takes us to new places we develop new friendships. We make friends at church. We get married and we become friends with our spouses' family and friends. All through life we will make lots of friends. Many will stay and many will go.

We need to recognize what we want out of a friend. We need to pray that God will send that perfect friend our way. Be specific in your prayer. Here are some of the things you may ask yourself when you consider what you want in a friend. Do you want?

- Someone that shares an interest in cooking or sewing.
- Someone that is athletic.
- Someone that shares your same religious background.
- Someone that has children the same age as your children.
- Someone with the same educational background.
- Someone with the same personality or with a different personality.
- Someone that I can truly be myself and that person will like me anyway.

- Someone that shares my same morals and ethics.
- Someone that does not like to drink or smoke.
- Someone that is not emotionally needy.

You get the idea, basically you know what you need in a friend so all you have to do is ask God.

My two closest friends live in different cities from me. So it is difficult to visit with them. I talk to them but I wanted a friend that lived in the same city as me. After my husband and I divorced, the children and I lived in an apartment. I wanted a Christian friend that had kids the same age as mine. I prayed that God would send the perfect friend my way. He answered my prayer. I had taken the kids to the pool in the apartment complex where we lived. There was a woman there with her teenage daughter. We started talking and quickly became good friends as did my children and her daughter. She was divorced too and we had a lot in common. We could talk about everything. When I met my husband, we no longer talked very much. Our friendship drifted away. I am friends with her on a social media site but we do not talk except occasionally on social media. She was a friend during a time when I needed it the most. God sent her my way during a difficult time in my life. We will have friends that last a lifetime and then there are friends that come into our life for a short time.

The Friendship Prayer

Dear God,

Everyone needs a friend. I am so thankful that I can come to You anytime I need to talk.

I ask for a friend that shares my same interest, values and morals.

I need a friend that I can laugh and cry with. Someone to lean on when there is sorrow and joy. Someone that is dependable and makes my burdens lighter just by being in my life.

I ask that you send a friend my way that is the perfect friend for me.

I pray that I will be a true friend to someone and they can rely on me in times of happiness and sadness.

I pray that I will show my children how to be a friend so they can nurture true friendships.

I ask all these things in Jesus name.

Amen.

The Career Prayer

Therefore, my beloved brethren, be ye stedfast, unmoveable, always abounding in the work of the Lord, farasmuch as ye know that your labour is not in vain in the Lord. (First Corinthians 15:58)

A woman's career is forever changing and being a mother with a career is always a challenge no matter the age of the child. Some women stop working to raise their children while others put their kids in daycare starting at age 6 weeks and they stay there until they are too old to attend. It does not matter which path you choose because once you become a mother everything changes.

Some mothers might choose to be a housewife so they can stay at home and care for the children and home. It is an admirable profession to be able to stay at home. Children feel secure and valued when the mother can be there after school. Back when I was a child, most mothers were stay at home mothers. Today, unless the man makes an incredible living, women work outside the home just to be able to put food on the table.

If you work outside the home, hopefully, you will be one of those mother's that has chosen a career that makes you very happy. When we have a secure job it shows in our demeanor. Children feel secure when the mother and father are happy in their chosen career.

As the economy changes so does a company's plans and resources. Many of us have found ourselves being laid off and many times. The job may stop but the bills keep coming. We update our resumes and pray that a job comes along quickly. If it takes several months to find a job, questions flood our minds such as:

How long can I survive before I lose my house? Can I feed my family? What happens if someone in my family gets sick? Will I be able to afford the doctor bills? What job will I be able to find? It does not matter if it is in my field just as long as I get a pay check. We need to remember that if our children see us in a panic about finances it worries them. They need to know that the parents have the money part of life under control.

You may find that you need to finish your college degree or attend a technical school. Whatever education path you choose all women need to obtain as much education as possible. You will be able to provide for your family better. When your child sees you trying to further your education, it motivates them to continue their education past high school.

Remember to lean on God and trust Him to guide your professional life.

The Career Prayer

Dear God,

I come before you today with much praise and thanksgiving for my job.

I ask that you will guide my actions each day at work. Help me to do the best job that I can every day.

I ask that you surround me with a boss and coworkers that share the same values, morals and ethics that I strive for daily.

I ask that I am eager to get to work each day so that I will perform my job to the best of my ability.

I pray that honesty and sincerity be in the front of my mind at all times. I want my actions to reflect to my boss and coworkers that they can trust me.

I pray that I will show respect to my coworkers.

I ask that through my actions they will see You.

I ask that I know how to guide my children to the right schools and assist them in choosing a career path that will make them happy and content. I ask that you show me how to direct my children in their professional life

I ask these things in Jesus name.

Amen.

A Prayer for Marriage

Wives, submit yourselves unto your own husbands, as unto the Lord. (Ephesians 5:22)

Therefore shall a man leave his father and his mother, and shall cleave unto his wife: and they shall be one flesh. (Genesis 2:24)

Being married to the perfect husband is a blessing. The idea situation is to marry the first person you date and you are married to that man till death do you part. My paternal grandmother said that we are supposed to marry the first man we date. I met a lady some years ago that told me she and her husband had never dated anyone else other than each other. I thought wow that is something that you almost never hear of in this day and time. As I talked to her I realized she was genuinely content and happy. Neither she nor her husband brought any emotional baggage into the relationship. She didn't have to think about her husband's exes and he did not have to be concerned about her exes. Their marriage is happy and carefree in that respect.

Many people, me included, are in a second marriage. Luckily for us each of our exes are wonderful people and we do not have problems on that part. When each one has children from a previous marriage there are many questions. Will the children get along? Will the husband and wife get along with their step children? There may be: tough financial times, health problems, leaky faucets, different taste in furniture and colors for decorating, rowdy kids, ailing parents, career changes and everything in between.

Through the years of marriage each person changes. Change can tear a marriage apart or make it stronger than ever. The important thing is to change together.

Having been married twice, I have learned a few things. Now I must interject here that even though one is trying very hard if the other one is not then the marriage could fail. Both man and wife should work together on the marriage. Key ingredients to a happy marriage:

Love each other!! When there is love in your heart for your husband then you will show love, kindness and a deep devotion to him.

50/50 day. Sometimes we think only about what we want, but we have a husband. Being selfish leads to disaster. We cannot only watch our favorite television shows or only cook what we like. Your husband might become very unhappy. Take turns with every day things. Make every day a 50/50 compromise. When it comes to meals, you may want chicken so let him pick the vegetable he wants. You may prepare his favorite dessert one week and then your favorite the next week. When it comes to daily chores, especially if both work outside the home, share in those chores. Your husband may always take out the trash and you may always clean the bathroom. Or you may take turns preparing the meals, vacuuming or dusting. In this way neither spouse becomes exhausted with household chores. When it comes to eating out, one week you pick the restaurant the next week he does. When it comes to entertainment, one time you pick a TV show to watch then he picks.

Communication. This one is huge. Talk, talk and talk!!! Talk about everything together. You are in this marriage together so you must communicate together. Even if the topic is uncomfortable you got to jump right in and talk it out.

Respect. No two people will think the same about every topic. Respect each other's opinions. I try not tell my husband he is wrong about his opinion. I do not want to be criticized for my opinions. For example, when we are in the car together sometimes I see this one car on the road that I think is the cutest car. I say, "That car is so cute." He says, "I think it is ugly." He does not tell me I am wrong for liking the car and I do not tell him he is wrong for disliking the car. Then we just laugh and laugh.

Laughing. I love to laugh. Try to find something to laugh about every day. Laughter puts a smile on your heart.

Forgiveness. When one person does something they should not, the other one must forgive. Then move past the transgression. It might be the most difficult thing you have ever done but for you to have a light heart forgiveness is the only way.

Honesty and trust. If you need to go to the store to buy your child some clothes and you know your budget is $200.00, then only spend what is in your budget. Your husband trust you to stick to the budget.

God needs to be a part of your marriage. I know that with work schedules that it is sometimes difficult but when all possible attend church together. Praying together will make the marriage strong.

When children see that their parents are working on having a good marriage it gives the child security. Pray that God will show you how to strengthen your marriage.

Do things together. When couples do not engage in activities together, they drift apart. Several years ago I met a woman who told me that she and her husband do not share interest in the same things. Even when they were on vacation she said they did their own separate activities during the day and would meet in the evening for dinner. I wonder if they are still married. Find something that you share an interest in it could be:

- Same taste in music
- Same interest in movies

- Hiking
- Running
- Antiquing
- Playing board games

I like to do scrapbooking so when I am working on that my husband will be in the same room as me but he is playing his guitar. We are not doing the same thing but we are together. We just laugh and talk.

A Prayer for Marriage

Heavenly Father,

I come to you today about my marriage. I love my husband and want to be a good wife.

I pray that the heart of my marriage is focused on You.

I pray that my love for my husband stays strong and grows deeper and stronger each day.

Help me to learn to compromise with my husband in all areas of our life.

Teach me how to communicate with my husband and him with me so that we are drawn closer together.

Teach me to respect his thoughts and opinions. Help me not to criticize him. Help me to realize that finding constant fault will tear the marriage apart. Help him to show me the same respect.

Humble my heart to forgive when he has done something wrong. I pray that he can forgive me when I have done something wrong.

Help each of us to be honest with each other so our marriage will be happy. Help each of us to have our words and actions be truthful.

In Jesus name I pray.

Amen

A Prayer for Respect

Let nothing be done through strife or vainglory; but in lowliness of mind let each esteem other better than themselves. (Philippians 2:3)

We have heard the phrase you must give respect to get respect. It is a very true statement. In the section of listening, I talked about listening to your children so they will feel valued. We need to take that a step further and show respect to our children. When your child comes to you with a problem, you may stand there focused on what they are saying but do you understand their situation?

Do you consider their words to be important? When your five year old comes to you crying because his toy broke, understand that his pain is very real to him. In our adult mind the problem can easily be solved but in a child's mind their whole world has been turned upside down.

Do you consider their words to be valuable? Do you go to your child and ask their opinion about a situation? Do you ask their opinion about a new dish you made for dinner? Even if she does not like the dish, she may tell you no but in a respectful manner. She sees that you value her opinion so she in turn will tell you the dish tasted bad but she will do it sweetly. Do you ask them if they had a good day at school?

How do you treat your child? Do you smile at your child? Do you do special things that you know will make your child happy? For example: you know that they had a difficult test at school so do you prepare their favorite after school snack? Do you ask them about their favorite foods, clothes, music and movies? Do you care about their interest? My daughter loved ballet. I was delighted taking her to classes and going to recitals. My son took karate and achieved a black belt. I enjoyed taking him to competitions. When my kids were in competitions, I could see that they were learning about respect, teamwork and it built their confidence.

Respect should extend to everyone in our lives. There are thousands of ways we can show respect to others so that our children will learn to respect themselves as well as others.

- When we respect our husband our child sees that their father is important, valued, and loved by their mother.
- Teaching our child to say "yes ma'am" or "no ma'am"
- Being polite to waiters, waitresses and store clerks
- Opening a door for either man or woman if they have their hands full.
- Helping a disabled person put groceries in their car
- Teaching your daughter to respect herself while out on a date
- Teaching your son to respect a woman
- If you say you will do something; do it! (we have all failed on this one)
- If your daughter hates the color blue, don't buy her a blue sweater
- If your son hates football don't push him to play just because your husband was the star quarter back

If you have difficulty in showing respect to anyone, pray that God will teach you how to respect that person.

A Prayer for Respect

Dear God,

I ask that you teach me how to show respect to my children.

Teach me to understand what my child tells me and to value their words. I want my child to feel valued and loved.

Help me to show respect to others even when I might not agree with their words or actions.

If I am having problems showing respect to someone, especially if they have done me wrong, show me how to let go of animosity, anger and remove that obstacle from my heart so that I can show respect.

I ask in Jesus name.

Amen

A Prayer of Contentment

Not that I speak in respect of want; for I have learned, in whatsoever state I am, therewith to be content. (Philippians 4:11)

How many of us can say that we are content with our lives? I am guessing not many of us. We are more than ever a society of "I want and I want it now." We are never satisfied with what we have. When a new electronic device hits the market we think we must go out and buy the next best thing. When styles change in fashion, we think that to be accepted we have to conform to what society says is in style.

I remember as a young mother, I was not content with anything in my life. I was sad because I did not have what I saw others have. I was happy for them with their nice possessions. I just wanted to be able to have those things too. I saw others with bigger houses, nicer furniture, and nicer cars and better dressed. Then I lived in a large house but it did not make me content. I have driven nice cars it did not make me content. I have dressed nice but it did not make me content.

But godliness with contentment is great gain. For we brought nothing into this world, and it is certain we can carry nothing out. And having food and raiment let us be therewith content. (First Timothy 6:6-8)

So what makes a person content with their material possessions? It comes from a desire deep in the heart to be content. I asked God to help me be content with what I have. He did! I would still like to have a bigger house but if I do not get one then that is okay. I look at my house and I am thankful. I do not look at it and feel sad because I do not have what others have. I am content. Contentment means you are satisfied with the things you have. It's not to say that you will never want for new things it just means you are okay with what you have right now.

Are you content with the people in your life? Is your husband a lawyer but you wished he was a doctor? Is someone in your life always running late or always early? Does it get on your nerves? Do you wish your daughter was a cheerleader instead of being in the band? Do you wish your son was smart in math and science but instead he wants to work on cars? Do you wish a family member would lose weight? These things can drive you crazy. Let it go. You cannot change the things that interest a person. You cannot change the jobs they choose. You cannot make a person look a particular way. The only thing you can change is your attitude toward a person.

Are you content with who you are as a person? Do you know how you feel about social issues such as: abortion, the death penalty, gun control, bullying, violent crimes, cybercrimes, fraud or theft? These are serious topics and morals, ethics, right and wrong are to be considered. Even among Christians people have different views. For example: gun control which seems we hear a lot about these days. Some people are strongly against having a gun anywhere close to them. They do not want them in their homes nor on their person. Other people have guns in their home and have a carry permit. Another example: abortion- many people believe it is a woman's right to choose whether she carries the baby to delivery or aborts. Others believe you should carry the baby to term regardless of the circumstances during conception. My point is, whatever your position is on these topics, be content with your views. Search your heart and know your mind. Pray that God will help you have the right attitude and outlook. Pray that your thoughts on these subjects are according to His will.

Do you know how you feel about simple topics such as: favorite restaurant, favorite TV shows, favorite color, and the best make up, the best stores or your favorite way to relax? It does not matter what the situation or issue, know what your thoughts are and admit to them. I am not talking about moral and ethical issues here or right and wrong situations. I am only referring to simple ordinary things. I love the color red. I can freely admit that I love to wear red. I am not going to suddenly say I don't like red because a friend says that she does not like red. If I said that I don't like red just to agree with her then I am not being true to myself. I would be dishonest with myself and the other person. This leads to constant dissatisfaction. Do not adopt other people's thoughts on something when you feel a different way because you will only be miserable and therefore not content.

You may find at times that you will be content and then a situation comes along and upsets your frame of mind. You may find yourself irritable, miserable and unsettled. It happens to everyone so do not fret. It is simple, just pray to God to restore you heart. He will every time.

At my grandfather's funeral, the minister said that he had a conversation with my grandfather a few months before he passed away. My grandfather told him that he had led a content life. That made a real impact on me. I began to think about what it meant to be content. I needed to learn to be content with my material possessions but I also needed to be content with heart and mind. The heart and mind is the tricky part. Over the years since my grandfather's death, I have slowly become content with many areas of my life. It is a work in progress. The key is to pray. If you need to be content with your home, car, career, friends, or the way you think about something just pray to God to teach you how to become content.

When our children see us as being content then it will show them how to be content. Pray that your children learn how to be content in all areas of their lives.

A Prayer of Contentment

Dear God,

I come to you today with a heavy heart. I pray that you will help me to be content with my material possessions and to be thankful for the blessings You have given me.

I have a house and because of my family I have a home.

I ask that you show me how to be content with my house, furnishing and vehicle and not constantly want what I cannot afford.

I have clothes on my back and shoes on my feet; show me to be content for these things as many do not have what I have. I praise you for supplying my needs and teach me to be truly thankful.

Help me to be content with my husband, children, parents and my extended family. You made each of us with a specific purpose in mind. I realize that none of us are perfect and I ask that You help me to appreciate them for the unique person they are.

Help me not to want to change them but to be content with each person. It is only then that I can have a peaceful heart.

I pray to be content with my emotions and the way that I look at things in life.

I pray for Your guidance in my thoughts, words, actions, and decisions each day so that I will be content.

I ask that each night as I go to bed that I can look back on my day and be content with what I see. I know that the contentment that I experience in my heart and mind only comes from you God.

I ask these things in Jesus name.

Amen.

A Prayer of Faith

Now faith is the substance of things hoped for, the evidence of things not seen. (Hebrews 11: 1)

How does this apply to our everyday life? We might not necessarily think about faith in terms of getting the kids off to school, our husband out the door to work, errands, meals, kids sports, homework, bills which is basically everyday life. We think about faith when we go to church. We have faith in God for our salvation. We have faith that Jesus died on the cross for our sins. Faith should not stop there. We need to take it further. As I stated we have faith in God for our salvation. We need to have faith in all areas of our lives. We need to have faith that God will answer our prayers.

And all things, whatsoever ye shall ask in prayer, believing, ye shall receive. (Matthew 21:22)

Each day is busy. Most of us try to put as many task in our 24 hours as we can. There are days when I do not get everything accomplished. There are days when I get it all checked off the list. Do not wait until you are on overload and feeling overwhelmed with your day before you go to God in prayer. Start the day with prayer that you will get the things done that needs to be done. Pray that God will guide and direct you in your day. Lean on Him.

Several years ago in the months of November and December I had a whirlwind of activities and I was not sure what I needed to do next. The last week of November my aunt and I gave my parents a 50th wedding anniversary party. Several days later was Thanksgiving. The second week of December I graduated with my Bachelor of Science degree. My parents gave me a graduation party. A few weeks later was Christmas and we had a house full of kids. To say I was busy would be putting it mildly. I felt overwhelmed. Why? I did not fully lean on God. I remember praying during that time but I did not have the kind of faith that I should have had. I should have leaned on God and laid all my troubles and concerns at his feet. I would have enjoyed all the activities a lot more than I did. I would have had a truly peaceful heart and I would have had the faith that everything would have gotten done.

A Prayer of Faith

Dear God,

Thank you for being loving and faithful to us. I praise you that I can turn to you each day. I have faith that you sent your Son Jesus to die on the cross for my sins.

Teach me to be have faith in You in all areas of my life. Help me to lean on You for guidance and direction in all situations.

Help me not to stress about the things that I cannot do anything about and fully have faith in You.

In Jesus name I pray.

Amen

A Prayer of Trust and Truth

Trust in the Lord with all thine heart; and lean not unto thine own understanding. (Proverbs 3:5)

It is a sad day when we become so jaded that we cannot trust what another person says to us. It is sad when a person walks around thinking that everyone is lying to them. Or, a person questions and analyzes every word that is said to them. I can only imagine what turmoil is in that person's heart. We have all lied and been lied to. Unfortunately, there are some people that we have gotten use to them telling us lies. Then we begin to think that everyone is lying. People that have never lied in the past suddenly we suspect them of altering the truth.

If your child tells you that they do not have any homework and they normally have homework, as a mother we will question that child. I am not particularly a fan of scare tactics but the child should know that you expect them to be truthful. You may even go so far as saying you will email their teacher. That is teaching your child that you expect them to be truthful. When your 17 year old daughter goes out on a date, you want to trust that she will do the right thing by being home on time. When she is home at the appointed time she is building your trust in her.

We want our children to have trust in us. When your child tells you something in confidence and she ask you not to tell and you promise not to tell. Don't tell. She might have confided in you that she no longer likes one of her friends. It might seem like a trivial thing to you but to her it is important. If she feels like she can trust

40

you on this issue then when a more serious situation arises she will confide in you.

Sometimes you must just trust that the other person will do the right thing. For example, when we tell someone that we will pray for them. Please keep true to your word. We trust that the person takes their words seriously. I know that for myself there has been times when I will say, "I will send you that recipe." Or, "I will call you and let you know that I made it home okay." I forget to send the recipe or because I am tired I may forget to call. Shame on me. Those little phrases that we speak so easily then never followed through cause people not to have confidence in us. Their trust in us breaks down.

We can always trust in God. He always gives us the truth. The Bible is one book that we can trust in and know that it is the truth. No matter what situation we are faced with we can open God's word and find the truth. We can be comforted by the knowledge contained within its pages.

A Prayer of Trust and Truth

Dear God,

I praise you dear Lord that I can trust your word completely. I know that you are faithful in your words.

I pray that you will guide me in being a person that others can trust.

I pray that the words that I speak are the truth.

I pray that my children will learn to trust in You.

I pray that my children will be the kind of people that others can trust.

I ask that others will see that they can trust in You.

In Jesus name I pray.

Amen

A Prayer of Joy and Happiness

This is the day which the Lord hath made; we will rejoice and be glad in it. (Psalm 118: 24)

You know the crazy thing is that when things are going great for us we seem to forget to give thanks and praise to God. We instantly go to Him in times of sadness, sorrow, sickness, death or when there is a big decision we need to make. But, we need to go to Him when everything is blissful. Let us think about everyday things that bring us an abundance of joy and happiness.

- Finding out you are pregnant
- The birth of your baby
- Your husband sending you flowers, just because.
- Buying a new house or car
- Hearing your child laugh out loud – the sweetest sound
- Seeing your flowers and /or vegetable garden grow
- Getting all the laundry done and the house cleaned
- Spending time with friends
- Hugs from your child
- Hugs from your husband
- A nice slow rain in the spring time.
- Sunshine any day of any season. It lifts the heart.
- The stillness of snow as it blankets the ground
- Good health
- Getting the job of your dreams
- Family or friends has had victory over a situation

- When someone has something spectacular happen to them
- Singing in church
- Smiles on someone's face when they see you
- Accomplishing a goal – walking a specific distance or reducing you television time.

Rejoicing in hope; patient in tribulation; continuing instant in prayer. (Romans 12:12)

A Prayer of Joy and Happiness

Dear God,

I come to you today with joy and happiness because _____
_____.
Thank You for showing me this joy in my life. I ask that I continue
to see all the things that You would have me to see and appreciate.
My heart is full of joy and happiness; I praise You and lift Your name
on high.

Thank You God for all this joy and happiness in my life.

In Jesus name I pray.

Amen.

A Prayer of Love

A new commandment I give unto you, That ye love one another;
as I have loved you, that ye also love one another. (John 13:34)

Love is wonderful, joyful, happy, and puts us on that euphoric high.
We have many types of love:

    Our love for God and Jesus

    Love for our husband

    Love for our children

    Love for our parents

    Love for our fellowman

The greatest love is God's love for us. The Bible tells us that God
is love. It is difficult to comprehend the immeasurable love that God
has for each of us. He loves us so much that He sent His Son, Jesus,
to die on the cross for the remission of our sins. Now that is love.

For God so loved the world, that he gave his only begotten Son,
that whosoever believeth in him should not perish, but have
everlasting life. (John 3:16)

God wants us to open our hearts and accept His love. We try
very hard to do everything right so that it is pleasing to God. We
fail. We are not perfect. Praise God, He loves us anyway.

But God commendeth his love toward us, in that, while we
were yet sinners, Christ died for us. (Romans 5:8)

Love is wonderful between a husband and wife. I briefly talked about love under the marriage section but I wanted to expand on love between a husband and wife. Love between a man and a woman is a deep emotion. A husband and wife are as one. We rely on each other. We trust each other with our thoughts. We know that our husband will protect us and he knows that we would protect him. I do not necessarily mean physical protection. Protection can be mentally and emotionally. We feel safe telling our husband our thoughts and he should feel safe telling you his thoughts. When you see each other after a long day at work, there is joy in being back together. You enjoy relaying the day's events. There is discussion about dinner, kids, money and family. Husband and wife are a team. You fall in love when you are dating. As the years pass, the love you experience grows deeper. You become comfortable with your life together. It is easy to become complacent. A couple must work on their marriage. Flirt with your husband. Go on a date with him. Work on the marriage.

Love is the deepest between mother and child. You think you have experienced love but when you have a child it takes love to a whole different level in our heart. When the doctor placed that baby in my arms my heart knew a whole different type of love. It does not take away from the love you feel for your husband, parents, siblings and family and friends. The heart expands and the love for that child is stronger than you could imagine. No matter how many children you have the heart grows larger so you can give your child all your love.

A Prayer of Love

Dear God most gracious Lord,

I come to you today in praise and thanksgiving for your love for me. My heart swells with gratitude.

I pray that you teach me to open my heart and mind to receive Your love. I pray that others can see Your love in me.

I pray for your guidance in teaching me to love my child unconditionally. My child is not perfect and does things that I may not always agree with. Teach me to love my child in the way that love will bring comfort and security in my child's heart. I pray that my child always feels my love.

I ask that you show me how to show love to my husband. Teach me to know how to relate to him in a positive manner that exhibits my love for him. Help him to be able to show me love in a way that brings us together stronger each day.

I ask that you guide me to be able to express my love for my family and friends. I pray that each person comes to You and accepts Your love.

I ask these things in Jesus name.

Amen

A Prayer for Laughter

A time to weep, and a time to laugh; a time to mourn, and a time to dance; (Ecclesiastes 3:4)

"Laughter puts a smile in your heart." As I like to say now.

I love to laugh. Every day I try to laugh about something. The sweetest laughter is the one that comes from your child. A child's laughter can be from playing peek-a-boo, reading their favorite story, or holding your child's hand while you twirl around. My favorite memory of my daughter laughing was when we were in Interlaken, Switzerland. It was 1986 and she was around 4 or 5 months old. We were at a restaurant in Interlaken. This particular area only had a restaurant. There were no other buildings around. We were fairly high up in the Swiss Alps so there was no traffic to be heard from the main highway below. There was only a two lane road that led to the restaurant. I had to change her diaper so I took her outside to the van. I noticed that there was no one outside in the parking lot. Just me and my daughter. I opened the back of the van and laid her down to change her diaper. After I took out the diaper and powder from the bag, I realized there were no sounds at all. There were no other people around, no sound from cars, nothing. It was one of those rare moments when there was total silence. I took off her diaper and I felt a little gust of wind. I guess the wind tickled her. She laughed out loud. Her laughter was the only sound I heard. It was the sweetest sound on earth.

Each day think of ways to laugh. Make it a point to have a light heart where laughter can easily enter your mind and heart. I am not saying that every moment will be constant laughter. That is unrealistic. What I am saying is that in the midst of a very hurried life that we all lead, laughter should be a part of your day.

> *Make a joyful noise unto the Lord, all ye lands. Serve the Lord with gladness; come before his presence with singing.* (Psalm 100:1-2)

I try to find some humor in various situations. When I was a teenager, my parents wanted me to help them paint the bottom grey blocks of the house to match the brick. The day I painted my section, my grandmother was with us and she wanted to be outside with me. So I got her a lawn chair and put it out there so she could talk to me while I painted. Our neighbor that lived across the street was outside and I noticed that he was standing at the end of his driveway watching my grandmother. I think all he could see was my grandmother sitting in a lawn chair talking to the end of the house. I do not think he saw me. I was on my knees painting the bottom of the house. He just stood there with his head tilted sideways. I can only imagine how funny it must have looked from his point of view. It makes me laugh whenever I think about it.

Not every situation will be a laugh out loud moment. Think of conversations with a family member or a friend that are pleasant. Relish the no drama conversations. Smile at the satisfying interaction.

I encourage you to look into your past and find events where you can see some humor. Then as things happen in your life you will begin to find the humor. Of course some things are normal everyday things that are not sad nor happy. It is just daily things. But when something out of the ordinary happens look to find some humor in it. Try to laugh. Then before you know it you will feel light hearted about many things that happen to you. You begin to let laughter into your heart.

A Prayer for Laughter

Dear God,

    I come to you today with a light heart. A heart that is full of joy, love, happiness and laughter.
    Help me to see the good in people.
    Help me to find comfort and joy in the small things in life.
    Help me to laugh so others can see that life is good.
    Fill my heart with gladness.
    In Jesus name I pray.

Amen

A Prayer for Sensitivity

And the peace of God, which passeth all understanding, shall keep your hearts and minds through Christ Jesus. (Philippians 4:7)

When it comes to being sensitive, balance is the key. Now when your child falls and scrapes his knee there is usually some tears involved. The child is not seriously hurt physically but mostly his feelings are hurt. You hear his whimper but as soon as he sees you for some reason he turns on the water works and the pain magnifies. You scoop him up in your arms while he wails and cries. You kiss his forehead and put a band aid on his knee. You tell him to be a big boy and you smile your biggest smile. He runs off to play and the pain of the knee is soon forgotten. You were sensitive for that small moment of trauma in his life.

There will be many situations where you will need to be sensitive to your child. There will be some little girl that will hurt your daughter's feelings. She will cry and cry. Your son will not make the ball team. You will tell him next time. Basically you are sensitive to your child which is a good thing. It will show him / her compassion, caring and kindness.

The other side of sensitivity can be a major problem. You have met all those people that are sensitive to everything. They question every word out of a person's mouth. They challenge every situation. These people try to catch someone in a lie. They want to make an issue out of every sentence you utter. They make you want to run away from them. For example: If you say to someone, "I don't like to eat chicken." Then a couple of months later you are at a friend's dinner party and you are eating a chicken dish and that person says to you in a sarcastic tone, "I didn't think you ate chicken." This person is trying to challenge you on something insignificant you said. This person is trying to trip you up. They want to rattle your mind and make you look like you have lied. Don't you just feel sorry for people like that? They must be very insecure and unhappy. For us Southerners we just say "Bless your heart."

When did we become a society of trying to constantly find fault with someone? When did we become self-conscious of every word we speak for fear of offending someone? It is because people have lost respect for others. They are not content. There is no trust, joy, love or happiness. People no longer have a light shining in their heart.

We want our children to be sensitive to others needs. We want them to show compassion and kindness. On the flip side we do not want them to be sensitive to the point they want to challenge and question every word that is said to them.

We need to pray for our children to be sensitive in a positive way. We want them to have a balance in their mind and heart when it comes to being sensitive.

A Prayer for Sensitivity

Dear God,

I come before you today in my search for sensitivity. I pray that I learn to have that balance in my heart and mind.

Help me to teach my child to be sensitive to others needs. I ask that they will become kind and caring in their daily walk with You.

I pray that I am not that person that questions and challenges every word that comes out of a person's mouth. Help me not to become critical and find fault.

Help me to teach my child not to question, challenge and find fault in others. Help me to be accepting of how others express their thoughts so I can show my child to do the same.

In Jesus name I pray.

Amen

A Prayer for Responsibility

For we must all appear before the judgment seat of Christ; that every one may receive the things done in his body, according to that he hath done, whether it be good or bad. (Second Corinthians 5:10)

I wonder why some people want to play the blame game. I suppose they cannot take responsibility for their actions because it is too difficult to accept mentally and emotionally. Obviously, if you drop a plate and as it hits the floor it breaks into about ten pieces you can say, "I dropped the plate." If you are by yourself you really cannot verbally blame someone but in your heart you blame your husband because he did not do the dishes that morning. Or you blame the kids because they piled the dishes too high. Bottom line you dropped the plate. Accept the fact that you dropped the plate and move on. Do not blame your husband or kids because of something they did or did not do. Be emotionally strong and say, "I dropped the plate." Then stop talking. Just take responsibility for your actions.

Now the plate example is fairly simple but it is the more serious issues we face that have people blaming everyone in their life. These people never accept responsibility for their actions. If they do something good then they want all the accolades and pats on the back. If they do or say something that is not so good then here comes the blame game.

For every man shall bear his own burden. (Galatians 6:5)

55

It is easy to admit I like chocolate. It is hard to admit that I watch too much television. I choose to sit in my recliner and turn on the television. I choose to eat cookies and drink milk while I watch my favorite shows. Now with those cookies and milk comes added weight. I did it. No one forced me to eat those cookies. I take responsibility for watching too much television and that I have been weak in my want to eat cookies.

Now there are harder things to take responsibility for in our life such as:

A dirty house: It is easy to blame everyone because your house looks like a cyclone hit. The typical blame is: the kids do not pick up their toys, my husband does nothing, I have an illness and do not feel like cleaning, or I work outside the home and there is not enough hours in the day to clean. Every person that lives in your house contributes to the mess. Make a list of chores for each person. Stick to it. If your house is a mess then admit that it is a mess. Take responsibility for your actions and do something about it if you want a clean house.

Not getting an education: Now I understand that money is a consideration on this one but there are student loans. I went to college after high school but did not finish. After my kids were grown I finished my degree. I could say the reason I did not finish back in the 80's was because I got married and we moved to Germany because my husband was in the Army. There were no online classes at that time. I could blame my husband because I did not finish. It was not his fault. I am the one that decided to quit school and get married. I take responsibility for that action in my life.

Take responsibility for your attitude: We get out of life what we put into it. Now there are times that things happen that is completely out of our control. People do things that affect us but it is how we react to their actions that will either make us stronger or break us. Take responsibility for your attitude. If you are accused of being hateful. Take a long look at your behavior lately. Ask God to show you where you have been hateful. Then as He answers your prayer and you see where you were hateful. The first step is to say, "Yes, I have been hateful." It can be very freeing to see where you made a mistake and to admit to your actions. Don't feel the need to justify why you were hateful unless the other person(s) ask for a reason. Sometimes when you feel the need to justify your actions you keep talking and talking and at one point the other person no longer believes you. It looks like you are trying to make excuses. Just own up to the fact that you were hateful. Then apologize for your actions and move on.

Pray that God will show you how to take responsibility for your actions. The first step is to admit your actions to yourself. That can be a challenge to admit when you have done something that you know you should not have done or, not done something you know you should have done. God will direct your path so you can see how to take responsibility for your actions.

A Prayer for Responsibility

Dear God,

Thank you for opening my eyes to my actions. It is difficult to admit when I have done something that I think someone else will find fault. I ask that you show and teach me how to take responsibility for my actions.

Show me how to teach my children to take responsibility for their actions. Help them to see when they take responsibility for their actions that it will make their heart lighter and their life will be peaceful.

In Jesus name I pray.

Amen

A Prayer When Things Change

Have not I commanded thee? Be strong and of a good courage; be not afraid, neither be thou dismayed: for the Lord thy God is with thee whithersoever thou goest. (Joshua 1:9)

Some people do not do well with change. Some people loves it when their lives are filled with constant changes. It rejuvenates their energy. It has always puzzled me that people do not adapt to change. Change is good. Children grow. They progress through school. They go to college. They fall in love and get married. They have babies. It is a cycle. I guess everyone expects those changes and accepts those easily. There are some changes that occur in our lives that makes more of a challenge to accept.

Divorce – Whether it is the husband or the wife that ask for the divorce, each person deals with changes. Even the spouse that ask for the divorce will experience sadness and loss. The spouse left standing in shock moves at a slower pace and does not know what to do with all the changes.

Death of a Family Member – Nothing shakes us and devastates us like a death in the family. It does not matter if the person has been sick or whether it was a sudden accident, it will cause deep seated pain that does not seem to subside. We have to deal with life without their presence. It is a major change.

Change of Jobs – If you have been the person that has unfortunately been laid off from a job, you know what a shock it is. There is fear of not finding another job. Let's say you find another job right away. You are faced with new coworkers, new job title, new hours, new insurance and benefits. Let's face it, everything is new and scary.

Buying a new house – It is exciting and fun to move to a new house. But it is a major change. The kitchen is laid out differently or the way you had the sofa and chairs suddenly cannot be the same way. These sound like silly things to some people but if you have lived in the same house for 20 years then you move, these changes can overwhelm us.

New marriage – If you find yourself in a second marriage, this is thrilling and an enormous change. You are learning to live with someone new. You have a new extended family. There is a lot to manage.

Empty nest– We have taken care of them for 18 years. He/she does not need us to take care of them. Now, they are ready to be an adult and follow their own path.

Regardless of the change we need to help our children adapt. They need to know that we support them. We need to pray for the ability to accept change.

A Prayer When Things Change

Dear God,

I come to You today with a change in my life _____

_____

Help me to accept and deal with this change. I ask that You teach me to handle this situation so that it does not over power my mind. Help me to put things in perspective so that I can discern the proper way to move forward.

I ask these things in Jesus name.

Amen

A Prayer about Criticism

A soft answer turneth away wrath; but grievous words stir up anger. (Proverbs 15:1)

When you criticize your children it can damage them to the point that it can negatively impact your relationship with your children. On the other hand, it can be the best thing for them. Why do we as mothers criticize our children so harshly? My thoughts are that because of our deep love for them we want them to be the best person they can be. When we see our children making huge mistakes we feel that we should talk to them about their choices. Now some kids take this criticism as a learning experience and whether they will admit it to their mother they are thankful for the direction. Now some kids take exception to every word that comes out of our mouth as a criticism.

Let us take examine the negative criticism. If you find yourself constantly criticizing your child regardless of what they do or say then I would advise you take a close look at why you are doing this. If are you doing this because you are unhappy? Examine your actions to discover why, so you can be open to improving. Or, is it because you find that the child constantly makes bad decisions. You may be unhappy with that child because you feel that their life is off track. It could be that you are unhappy with the child's choices or it could be that your personality is so opposite of your child's that there is constant conflict.

I am sure all of you have heard the phrase 'pick your battles?' Well, that is certainly true when criticizing your child. If you criticize everything don't be surprised when your child withdraws from you as he / she gets older. For example, making the bed, so what if the comforter / bedspread is not perfectly placed on the bed. What is the big deal? It is not as if someone will report you to the house cleaning police. So what if your child loves to wear a particular shirt that you find hideous. They are expressing themselves. I know because many a time I had to step back and think these things are trivial. This time next year will that poorly made bed or the hideous shirt really be that important? Now let us go to the far end of that spectrum and look at moral and ethical issues. For example, if your child is rude and mean to everyone, starts stealing, cheats on test or physically hurts people such as in bullying. It is our responsibility to speak to our child regarding their behavior.

Constructive criticism if done in a loving tone will help your child become a better person. For example, your child wants to go to college but cannot make up his/her mind on where to attend. You know the deadline is approaching to submit their application. You may remind them that if they want to attend one of the better schools they need to make a decision.

Sometimes it does not matter what you say to your child the child sees it as a criticism. You may think of it as giving direction such as: why don't you wear the pink blouse it looks better on you than the yellow one. Your daughter may view it as a major criticism but you view it as giving a suggestion. This is where you will need to know your child and how well they accept a suggestion. If you know this about your child you may need to modify how you approach him/her. This goes back to the communication section.

Pray that God will teach you not to criticize.

A Prayer about Criticism

Dear God,

I pray that You will teach me not to criticize my child in a negative way that will cause them emotional harm.

I pray that my child will see that the guidance I give is because I love them so much that I want him/her to make the best decisions.

I pray that You show me how to let go of the issues that are not really that important. Then when there is a serious issue my child will be open to receiving my guidance.

I ask that my child will open their heart and mind and not get upset when guidance is given.

I ask these things in Jesus name.

Amen

A Prayer when there is Anger

Wherefore, my beloved brethren, let every man be swift to hear, slow to speak, slow to wrath. For the wrath of man worketh not the righteousness of God. (James 1:19-20)

Anger is a powerful emotion. It can consume every part of our daily life. We can be angry with ourselves and or angry with someone else. Sometimes the anger can be both at the same time.

When we have anger toward ourselves, there are always other emotions that hit us in combination with the anger. We can have feelings of shame and embarrassment that always seem to accompany the anger. We can be angry with ourselves because we did something we should not have done or because of something we did not do and knew we should. We may become angry with ourselves because, we did not do our best in school so that impacts our ability to find that perfect job. We may become angry with ourselves because we have not taken good care of our bodies. There is weight gain, stop wearing makeup, letting our hair go by not getting haircuts, wearing sloppy clothes because we are too lazy to do better. A person may have an addiction problem such as, cigarettes, drinking, drugs, gambling, stealing, affairs, harassment, temper, dishonesty, or cursing. It is easy to become angry with ourselves when we are doing things that we should not do.

When we are angry with another person, it seems to hurt worst because those feelings usually bring feelings of betrayal, sadness and heart aches. We must watch ourselves because the anger can fester in our hearts and before we realize it that anger has embedded itself so deep inside that it is difficult to move past it.

As mothers we can become angry when our child does not do well in school. We are angry because we know that they have not lived up to their full potential. We get angry with coaches or teachers if we feel that our child has not been treated fairly. When our child makes choices that makes no sense to us, anger surfaces in our heart. If those choices are not morally and ethically good, we have a difficult time making sense of their choices, anger slips in our heart. (see section on criticism). We have such a deep love for our child that we just want all their choices to be good. Our child will make stupid choices and they may wear funny clothes and dye their hair some strange color that just makes us roll our eyes but, we still love them.

Bottom line, we all get angry. The question is how we deal with that anger. We must give the problem to God.

A Prayer when there is Anger

My Heavenly Father,

I come to you today with a heavy heart that is full of anger because _____.

I give this burden over to you to release the pain from my mind and heart.

Teach me to deal with this problem in a positive way. Show me the way I should think about all the trials and tribulation that may come my way. Help me to process things in my heart and mind that will bring You all the glory and praise.

In Jesus name I pray.

Amen

A Prayer for Worry, Fear and Negativity

And the peace of God, which passeth all understanding,
shall keep your hearts and minds through Christ Jesus.
(Philippians 4:7)

It is human nature to worry about things. Then fear and negativity creep into our thoughts. I am a worry wart and I have fears. It is not an easy thing to admit. I think when we worry and have fear it is the absence of faith.

Do you, like myself, have worries and fears over things that feels like the world is falling apart then a month later that fear suddenly becomes trivial? We wonder why we even worried at all. Nothing worries us more than our children's well being. When our child is sick fear and worry comes to the front of our mind tenfold. We worry when it is a simple cold or sinus infection. Then when the child falls and breaks an arm we look back and think why did I worry about a little cold.

Fear can come in different forms. There are fears of spiders, snakes, dogs, tornados, hurricanes, sinkholes, earthquakes, or being a victim of a crime. Many people have a fear of some or maybe all of these that I have listed. Then there are some fears that we have but people might not talk about them. People may have a fear of being in a room with many people. Someone may fear making someone mad so they agree with whatever someone says. Some people have a fear that they are always being judged by the things they say or do because they have been criticized so much.

Fear thou not; for I am with thee: be not dismayed; for I am thy God: I will strengthen thee; yea, I will help thee; yea, I will uphold thee with the right hand of my righteousness. (Isaiah 41:10)

Worry and fear produces negativity. For example: the person that fears they will make someone mad may stop going to church, family gatherings, or any social setting. They have negative thoughts that everywhere they go they will make someone mad so they withdraw from all the important people in their lives.

Whatever worries, fears, or negative thoughts that enter our mind we can be set free from those thoughts through laying them at the feet of Jesus. We need to trust God completely to meet all our needs. He will do it plain and simple.

A Prayer for Worry, Fear and Negativity

Dear God,

I cast my worries, fears and negative thoughts to you. I lay my troubles at your feet.

When I worry, help me Lord to have faith in You. I know that there is no need to worry about things that have not happened or that I cannot do anything about. It only hinders my faith in You.

When fear creeps into my mind, I pray that all my fears are replaced with joy, love and happiness.

When negativity cripples my thoughts, I ask that those thoughts be turned into positive affirmations.

Teach me to trust in You and Your love and guidance.

In Jesus name I pray.

Amen.

A Prayer of Sadness and Loss

Blessed are they that mourn: for they shall be comforted. (Matthew 5:4)

Sometimes we encounter situations that brings great sadness and loss that seems to overwhelm us. The pain in the heart and mind can seem too great to bear. There may be a time when the light at the end of the tunnel seems so far away. You may even wonder if there will be joy in your life again. I know that I cannot even begin to imagine all the troubles that are out there that all mothers face but here are a few that come to mind.

- Death of a child - it is the deepest pain a mother can experience
- Death of a spouse, parent, sibling or other close family members
- Loss of a job
- Loss of a home
- Too many house repairs
- A friend turning their back on you
- Being in a car wreck
- Bad health of your child, husband or yourself
- Too many bills
- Not enough money for food
- Crime – burglary, rape, viciously attacked, theft, identity theft, etc.
- Child not doing well in school

- Discipline problems
- Not being able to motivate your child

When everything seems to come at us at once it seems impossible to come out of the sadness. There is always a light at the end of the sadness and loss. If you are faced with incredible sadness and loss find something that brings you comfort and use that in combination with your prayer to God. For example: standing out in the sun brings warmth and comfort, taking a long walk can help you feel like you are releasing your troubles, or taking a warm bath can feel like you are cleansing you mental state. Whatever you do to relieve the sadness, in the midst of it lift your eyes toward heaven and pray.

Trust in Jesus because he will carry your burden.

A Prayer of Sadness and Loss

My heavenly Father,

I come to you today with a heavy heart that is burdened with

I lay this burden at Your feet. I ask that You carry these troubles for me. My load is heavy and only You can make it lighter. Heal my broken spirit. Give me strength to endure these troubles. Comfort and restore my heart and mind.

I ask all these things in Jesus precious and holy name I pray.

Amen.

A Prayer on Guilt

If we confess our sins, he is faithful and just to forgive us our sins, and to cleanse us from all unrighteousness. (First John 1: 9)

When a person carries guilt around it can feel like a boulder has permanently attached itself to our shoulders. Guilt comes in many different forms. Let me explain what I mean by that, the worse the crime the worst the level of guilt we heap on ourselves. If you take the last cookie from the box there may be guilt because you know deep down your child would like it but it is the last one in the box. You really, really want it and hey it is your favorite. You eat the cookie and feel a small amount of guilt. You rationalize it because you are going to the store the next day and you will buy another box. As soon as you buy that new box and you give your child a cookie the guilt goes away. We tell ourselves that no one knew about it and we did not hurt anyone. The only person it hurt was you. You felt guilt. You say it was only a cookie. Yes, it was but if you felt guilt then you did something you were not supposed to do.

Then there are those words that we spoke and cannot take back. I remember when I was a teenager we had a neighbor that was very rude and hateful. She could be nice at times though. One day our family was eating dinner and the phone rang. In those days no caller id so I answered the phone and it was the neighbor lady. I was extremely rude to her. I do not recall my exact words but I told her that we were eating dinner and that she could call back later. My parents were not happy with me and they admonished me as well as they should. She treated me differently after that; she was actually nicer to me. I never apologized to her although I felt guilt for speaking to her so rudely. There was no excuse for my words and actions. When I got married she helped give me a bridal shower. She had gotten mellow over the years I guess. She passed away when my oldest child was around ten or so. I never took my opportunity to apologize to her. I had plenty of chances over the years but I never apologized. Even now after writing this story I feel guilty because I made a person feel bad. I hurt her feelings. I prayed just now for forgiveness. A chunk of the boulder just broke away.

There are millions of things as mothers that we have done or not done that will make us feel guilty. We do the best we can. Because of fear that our child will get seriously hurt we may not let our child participate in football or hockey. And when you son looks at you with pain in his eyes because he cannot play you will feel guilt. When your daughter wants to go to a technical school instead of a traditional college, you insist she go to college. She cries that it is not what she wants to do with her life. She seems sad and guilt enters the mind. All mothers have guilt about something. It is difficult to know all the right things to say and do. That is why it is so important that we pray for guidance.

A Prayer on Guilt

Dear God,

I come to you because I have emotions of guilt because I _____
_____ Help me
to understand what I have done in this situation. Help me to learn
from my mistake and not to repeat my offense.

Show me how to release the guilt from my heart so that I do not
have this heaviness on me.

Help me to learn from my sins and mistakes so that I will not
repeat them.

In Jesus name I pray.

Amen

A Prayer for Forgiveness

And be ye kind one to another, tenderhearted, forgive one another, even as God for Christ's sake hath forgiven you. (Ephesians 4:32)

We have all done or said something to someone that needs to be forgiven. We cannot please everyone all the time and there is no need to even try. The only person we make unhappy is ourselves.

There are times that we as mothers need to forgive and be forgiven. First, let us talk about our need to forgive. When the child yells at us and calls us stupid, forgive. If your mother or father does not respect you, forgive. If your brother never calls you, forgive. If your grandmother calls you fat, forgive. You might not know all the reasons behind why a person does or says the things they do. We might truly understand if we walked a mile in their shoes. There are things outside of the mother child relationship that happen to us that we need to forgive. For example:

- Your husband may say something to you that hurts your feelings
- You might be passed over for a promotion
- Your best friend may not invite you to a dinner party
- Family and friends may not respect your thoughts and opinions
- People may insult your children

Second, we want to be forgiven. You might turn your son's underwear pink by mistake. You want to be forgiven. You might forget to tell your daughter that the boy she has a crush on called her. You want her to forgive you. We want to be forgiven when we make mistakes.

>*For all have sinned, and come short of the glory of God.* (Romans 3:23)

Here is the best part. When you have done or said something wrong, God will forgive you. All you have to do is ask God to forgive you of all your sins.

>*If we confess our sins, he is faithful and just to forgive us our sins, and to cleanse us from all unrighteousness.* (First John 1:9)

A Prayer of Forgiveness

Dear God,

I come to you today with my burdens and heartache. I have committed a sin, _____

I ask that you forgive me for my sin. I know that this was wrong and I am sorry for my sin. Help me to control my words and actions so that I can glorify You Lord.

I ask in Jesus name.

Amen.

A Prayer of Health

Beloved, I wish above all things that thou mayest prosper and be in health, even as thy soul prospereth. (Third John 1: 2)

I have always heard that if you have your health you have everything. Nothing puts us in crisis mode than with the news that a loved one or our self has a health problem. We automatically begin to pray and ask others to pray also.

I have had my fair share of health problems. Nothing life threatening so I am very thankful for that but I live daily with physical pain. I have endured that for over thirty years. I have tried very hard not to become bitter. The doctor who delivered me was a country doctor that basically had no idea what he was doing. He allowed me to stay in the breech position too long. He should have sent my mother to a larger hospital so they could perform a C-section. He did not. I forgive the doctor for not being smart enough to send my mother to a more qualified doctor. Since I stayed in the breech position for so long, by the time I was born I had a dislocated hip and a fractured spine. It took three months to discover the hip being out of place. At that time they put me in a cast then a brace. By the time I was a teenager my left leg was about 2 inches shorter than my right. In my mid-forties I had my hip replaced. Several years later I had a fusion on my spine. I am 90% better but there are days when the pain can be pretty bad. When the pain becomes unbearable, I have on occasion become angry. The severe pain and anger goes away in a day or two. I have not questioned God on why I must endure this pain. I know there is a reason. I accept it.

Have you ever looked at someone and thought they are the picture of health? Only to find out that they have something horrible that they are dealing with. You think oh my goodness I had no idea. I could not handle what they are going through. That person probably looks at you or me and after learning of our problems says the same thing, I could not handle what she is going through. Suddenly our own problems do not seem so bad.

The hardest time of a health crisis is when it involves your child. When my son was three, he was diagnosed with Spinal Meningitis. I prayed and prayed that my son would be okay. The doctor, with tears in her eyes, told me that there was a possibility that one of three things would happened to my son. She said he could be deaf, he could become mentally challenged, or he could die. I was devastated. I continued to pray that God would heal his body. God answered my prayer. My son recovered with no permanent damage. Today he is a healthy young man that is a Staff Sergeant in the United States Air Force.

Regardless of the health problems you are facing, take those health concerns to God in prayer.

A Prayer of Health

Dear God,

I come to you with a health concern. I or _____ have /
has been diagnosed with _____.

You are the almighty physician and healer. I ask that you heal
this affliction. I ask that you guide me/us to the best doctor. Help
them to find the best treatment so I/or (loved one) can be healed.
I pray that will wrap your loving arms around me and teach me
patience, strength and courage to make it through this ordeal. I
pray that I can see hope when things get difficult to endure. I know
that you will not give me more than I can carry.

I ask these things in Jesus name.

Amen.

A Prayer for the United States of America

If my people, which are called by my name, shall humble themselves, and pray, and seek my face, and turn from their wicked ways; then will I hear from heaven, and will forgive their sin, and will heal their land. (Second Chronicles 7:14)

We are privileged to live in the United States of America. It truly is a great nation. I have had the opportunity to travel to many European countries. They were breathtakingly beautiful. I have great memories of my time over there. I have seen the Eiffel Tower in France, the Swiss Alps, I have seen Neuschwanstein Castle in Germany, the wind mills in Holland, the Vatican in Italy. However, nothing is more wonderful than coming back to the United States. I remember how my heart swelled with pride when the plane was over the United States. I am proud to be an American and I hope that you are too.

Our founding fathers had a great vision for our country. They wanted the people to be able to voice their thoughts and opinions about our government. They wanted us to be a part in the say on how the government was run. I feel both privileged and honored that my children have grown up in the United States of America.

There have been great presidents and there have been those that were not that great. Regardless of mine or your opinion of our government, we must continue to pray that those that are in power will do what is right and good. We should ask God to lead them in making right decisions for our country. We should pray that God will direct their path and that the leaders will want to do what is best for our country.

A Prayer for the United States of America

Dear God,

Thank you for allowing me to live in our great nation. I pray for our leaders in government that they will make good solid decisions. Show them the right path they should walk so that You will be honored.

I ask these things in Jesus name.

Amen.

A Prayer for the Military

Greater love hath no man than this, that a man lay down his life for his friends. (John 15:13)

As I have stated earlier, my son serves in the Air Force. I am so proud of him and his service to our country.

We have five branches of services.

Air Force
Army
Coast Guard
Marines
Navy

Each branch is vital in the protection of our country. It is because of our military that we get to enjoy our freedom. We get to enjoy the freedom of speech, religion (we are free to attend any church), we can choose our career, we can go to the store anytime we choose, we can go on vacations and we can attend events without fear of punishment. It is a huge sacrifice that each man and woman makes when they join the military. Yes, they did choose to join the service but that shows their commitment to their country. They are away from their families for long periods of time. They cannot go home any time they wish. It is an adjustment on the service member and the family. Being in the military is dedication, courage, honor, and commitment.

Personal note: I would like to thank each man and woman that has served in any branch of the military. I appreciate your service to our country.

A Prayer for our Military

Dear God,

Thank you for each man and woman that has made the commitment to serve in the military.

I ask that you give each one the confidence to perform their task assigned to them. I pray that you would comfort their mind because their jobs are dangerous and stressful.

I pray that you wrap your loving arms around them to keep them safe.

I ask that you be with their families as they struggle because their loved one is away. Give them comfort and strength.

I ask these things in Jesus name.

Amen.

A Prayer at Christmas

And she shall bring forth a son, and thou shalt call his name JESUS: for he shall save his people from their sins. (Matthew 1:21)

I love Christmas. It is a magical time of the year. It seems that stores put out the Christmas decorations earlier and earlier every year. They put out all types of merchandise that is Christmas themed. They give us huge discounts and specials. The Christmas trees are elaborately decorated. It is supposed to put us in the buying mood and the bigger the sales the more we buy. It puts us in the Christmas spirit. We buy more at the grocery store because we bake and cook more than normal. As you drive around at night people have the outside of their homes decorated. It completes our Christmas experience.

There is more food around the house than normal. The turkey, ham, sweet potatoes, any variety of vegetables and of course the many cakes, pies and other desserts. During the meal time, there is always love and laughter. It is so special to share with family at Christmas. Everyone is in a good mood and the sentiment shared is love.

When the kids are home for Christmas, we put up a tree, lights on the outside of the house, a village, and various things that I set around the house. I love buying presents for my family. Over the past couple of years we have gotten in the habit of giving each other cash and/or gift cards. I remember as a kid and even in my early adult years there was no such thing as a gift card. We bought actual presents. Then on Christmas Day we would exchange gifts. The children's eyes danced with excitement. The adults too although they probably would not admit to it. Oh, the thrill of it all.

I, along with most people I would guess, get caught up in the commercial part of Christmas. I find myself while I am decorating, baking, wrapping presents get a tug in my heart that tells me to stop and think about Jesus. I think about his birth and how God gave us the ultimate gift, His Son Jesus. The greatest love shared with us is the love that God has for us. That love is so strong that he sent his Son Jesus to be born of a virgin, Mary. Christmas is the celebration of Jesus's birth. The story of Jesus birth can be found in Luke 2: 1-21.

I encourage you as you begin your Christmas preparations that you remember the reason for the celebration. Remember God's love for us. Remember Jesus's birth. My heart rejoices as I think about how great His love is for us that he sent his only Son so that we might have eternal life. Now that is a reason to celebrate!!

A Prayer at Christmas

Dear God our Divine Heavenly Father,

I come to you today in praise and thanksgiving that you sent your Son Jesus to be born of a virgin, Mary.

I ask that I always remember that the day of celebration is about the birth of Jesus.

I pray that I not get caught up in the commercial aspect of Christmas.

I pray for those that do not have a family to celebrate with that you will send them peace and comfort.

I pray for those that have never heard of Jesus that you will send someone in their life to tell them of His love.

I pray for peace and love to surround my family and friends as we celebrate this special time of the year. My heart is full of love and joy because Jesus lives in my heart. I pray all these things in Jesus's name.

Amen.

A Prayer at Thanksgiving

In every thing give thanks: for this is the will of God in Christ Jesus concerning you. (First Thessalonians 5:18)

We all love Thanksgiving because most people are off from work on Thursday which is Thanksgiving and also the Friday after, which gives a long weekend.

Thanksgiving Day is usually with family and filled with more food than anyone could imagine. If a person is really brave on Friday, they are at the stores in the wee hours of the morning to get those mega sales. It is the kick off to the Christmas season. Now on Facebook, starting in November each person is to post something they are thankful for each day up to Thanksgiving Day. I have often wondered why we are not thankful all year long for all the things that are important to us. I think most of us are thankful but Thanksgiving time reminds us that we should focus on all the things that are important to us. It brings those things to the front of our minds. Think of all the things that are important to you. The things that I am most thankful for are:

God and that he sent His Son Jesus to die on the cross for our sins. He paid the price for me and for you. That is amazing.

My children – I have a daughter and son.

My husband

Step children

Step grandchildren

My parents

Aunts, uncles and cousins

Friends
Church and church family
My home
Car
Furniture
Clothes and shoes
Having a Job
Great co-workers
Freedom
All the military branches, Air Force, Army, Marines, Navy
and Coast Guard
Rain and Snow
Hugs and Kisses
Music
Flowers
Sunshine
Soft breezes
Laughing
Plenty of food
Friendly face or voice
Meeting new people
Kindness of a stranger
Smiles
Words of encouragement
Maybe seeing a place for the first time – Grand Canyon,
Niagara Falls, the ocean

Sometimes when I pray, the entire prayer is about all the things
that I am thankful for. It is a prayer of praise that God sent us his
Son. Then I tell Him all the things I am thankful for. The peace in
my heart is overwhelming. Please give it a try.

A Prayer of Thanksgiving

Dear God,

I want to thank you and praise you for sending your son Jesus. My heart is overflowing with praise that Jesus died on the cross for my sins. I give You all the glory.

I thank you for my children. They are so sweet and have given me so much joy and love.

I pray that I give them love, support and encouragement.

Thank you for my husband. I am thankful for someone to share my daily life with. I am thankful for my family and friends.

I am thankful for (list everything you are thankful for). My life is over flowing.

In Jesus name I pray.

Amen.

A Prayer at Easter

And he saith unto them, Be not affrighted: Ye seek Jesus of Nazareth, which was crucified: he is risen; he is not here: behold the place where they laid him. (St. Mark 16:6)

Easter is the time of year that we celebrate the death and resurrection of Jesus. Luke 23:1-43 tells us of Jesus crucified. Luke 23:44-56 tells us of this death. Luke 24: 1-50 tells of His resurrection and ascension. Jesus knew it was God's plan for Him to die on the cross. He realized what He was about to endure. He knew of the pain of being nailed to the cross. He did it for you. He knew of the agony and suffering He was to face as He hanged on the cross. He did it for you. Jesus was willing to pay the price for our sins. He took our place on that cross. Then He rose. Can you imagine their surprise when they could not find Him? Then He ascccended into Heaven. My heart swells in awe and wonder of the love that God has for us that He sent His only son, Jesus, to die on the cross for our sins.

Easter eggs, chocolate bunnies, new Easter clothes and everything is new at Easter and the spring time. The leaves come out, the grass turns green, flowers bloom and we feel a sense of hope of all things new. Each year when Easter and spring time come around, smile and let your heart be filled with hope, love, comfort and peace.

A Prayer at Easter

Dear God,

Thank you for sending Jesus to die on the cross for our sins. I am in amazement of your wondrous love for us. As we celebrate Easter, show and teach us to focus on the death and resurrection of Jesus.

In a world that does not know you, I pray that they will humble their hearts and realize that Jesus died on the cross for their sins. I pray they will invite You into their hearts.

I praise you that because of Jesus I can see a future full of love, hope, and peace.

I ask that each person recognizes that Jesus is God's son and that He died on the cross for the remission of our sins. We praise and honor You.

In Jesus name I pray.

Amen

My Prayer of Salvation

I was about 10 years old and one night at home my mother was sewing and I was watching television and a very poplar evangelistic preacher was on. I really listened to his message. I began to think about heaven and hell. I came to the age of accountability which brought on a heavy heart. I realized that I was a sinful person. I knew that I needed Jesus to come into my heart. I remember crying and thinking if I died I would spend eternity in hell.

January 13th 1974, I was at church. Our pastor was preaching and during his sermon I began to have a burden on my heart. I felt the weight of sin. I realized what having a sinful nature meant. When the invitation was given I made my way down to the altar. I knelt at the altar and began to pray. Now as a young girl of 10 years old I did not know how to pray except as a little child. This is what I prayed.

"Lord, please do not lift me down but lift me up into the Kingdom of Heaven and take away all my sins"

I remember knelling at the front pew. I was so focused on my prayer I did not hear the congregation leave. I kept praying over and over. I knew that I wanted Jesus to come and live in my heart. I kept asking for Jesus to come into heart. I waited and waited patiently. Then, I saw a light that started at the top of my head. That light slowly moved down past my eyes and down to my heart then filled my entire body. Jesus filled my heart. I raised my head and the only people left in the church was my mother, the preacher and his wife. That particular day in January, it was a cold, grey and dreary day. The sun did not shine that day. However, I saw the sun shine inside the church. I asked if they saw the sun and they said no. For me it was a beautiful sun shined filled day. The peace in my heart was beyond words.

The following week I joined the church. The next week I was baptized during the evening service.

If you have not accepted Jesus into your heart as your Savior I invite you to do so.

> *That if thou shalt confess with thy mouth the Lord Jesus, and shalt believe in thine heart that God hath raised him from the dead, thou shalt be saved.* (Romans 10:9)

Printed in the United States
By Bookmasters